OVER
YONDER

ALSO BY GLENIS REDMOND

Praise Songs for Dave the Potter

The Listening Skin

The Three Harriets and Others

What My Hand Say

Under the Sun

Backbone

The Song of Everything

Take Note

OVER YONDER

GLENIS REDMOND

GOOD PRINTED THINGS

Edited by Ashley Crout
Cover Art by Alexander Rouse
Book Design by Lib Ramos

First Edition

Printed in the United States of America
goodprintedthings.com
Greenville, South Carolina

ISBN: 978-1-7345844-9-3
LCCN: 2025939285

For my grandma, Katie Latimore (1901–2010),
my grandchildren—Julian, Paisley, and Quinn—
and for grandparents and grandchildren everywhere.

"Be like water making its way through cracks.
Do not be assertive, but adjust to the object,
and you shall find a way around or through it."

— *Bruce Lee*

"Life is not measured by the number
of breaths we take, but by the moments that
take our breath away"

— *Maya Angelou*

"If certain, when this life was out—
That yours and mine, should be
I'd toss it yonder, like a Rind,
And take Eternity—"

— *Emily Dickinson*

TABLE OF CONTENTS

FOREWORD

Let me tell you about what happened to Glenis Redmond's face when I saw her smile: I saw a deep pond, water dark and peaceful. It was daytime, but cloudy, as these recent days so often are, but as I looked into that calm black water, the sun outshone the clouds. The pond brightened, and it seemed that the light had been inside the water all along. So bright! So deep. So beautiful. That smile, that whole-face, full-glow smile. When Glenis Redmond talked about this new book, her whole self became a smile. I love to see a Black woman smile.

Over Yonder: A Poet's Exploration of South Carolina's State Parks is a project of love. That's why Glenis Redmond smiled so completely when she told me she'd nearly finished this book. So much love inside these pages. First and foremost, a Gaga's love for her grandson. For all her grandchildren. That grandmother's (Redmond's) memory of the love she received from her own grandmother as well. Redmond's love for her own children. Intergenerational love in all these pages.

Her love for her mother and grandmother. The bountiful blessing Redmond's mother received from Redmond's grandmother as well. These poems are stitched through with familial care and love, much like the quilts referenced in the Afro-Carolinian Quilt Stitch form Redmond introduces in these pages.

And there's the love of the land and the plants and animals and the waterways, the love of the sounds and sites of the parks in the state she calls home. Completing this book, Redmond achieved her mission of visiting every State Park in South Carolina, and some bonus sites as well. This was a quest that becomes more remarkable when we learn that within the author's own lifetime, it was illegal for Black people to visit many of these state parks. With a caring attention to detail, Redmond teaches her reader new things about the place she calls home. History and the present fold together in these poems. Sometimes sad and cruel history. Sometimes scary facts about our current times. But always, when observed and reported by Redmond, we are shown the necessary, unavoidable truth about the place where she lives and all those who live there. I've learned so much from *Over Yonder* about what it means to live in a state where—for at least the length of a walk outside in a park—I can be fully and vibrantly alive. When I finished *Over Yonder*, I couldn't help but smile.

— *Camille T. Dungy, author of* America, A Love Story *(Wesleyan UP) and editor of* Black Nature: Four Centuries of African American Nature Poems *(UGA Press)*

INTRODUCTION

Over Yonder: A Poet's Exploration of South Carolina's State Parks is book two of a collection of poems inspired by my State Park excursions with my grandson, Julian. I will admit to this candidly. It is easier to get a five-year-old to go to the park than it is to convince a tween to go. He is now ten to my sixty-one. Age has changed us, but still we go. Sometimes I go solo when he cannot be persuaded or when I am on a poetry tour. I relish when we are together because the sights and wonders land differently. We went to all 47 South Carolina State Parks—an achievement that officially makes us "Ultimate Outsiders." But beyond the title and the miles we've traveled, this journey is about far more than ticking parks off a list. Though list-ticking is satisfying to this Type A, Virgo woman.

Getting outside of our everyday routines to go Over Yonder like my grandmother, Katie Latimore, would advise was the point. She was not talking about the state parks, as she never visited one, but she did believe in what she called the *old ways*, which included the land and nature.

She would tell me to be close to the land as a teen, but I barely knew what she meant. Still I knew her words contained both wisdom and medicine in them. Yet I must have always known what my Grandma meant because I have always been an outdoors girl. I was a Brownie and a Girl Scout. I was a tomboy who loved playing outdoors. From ages 5 through 9, my Mama was always calling me home. I was out there somewhere high in a tree in the woods or just sitting on the curb outside in front of our house. Unlike my Mother and Grandmother, I always knew the names of birds, trees and flowers. No one taught them to me. I just knew. I grew a garden unassisted at age 11 in rocky Italian soil in our Vajont backyard.

My Grandma meant for me to get out in nature by not just tending to the land, but letting the land tend to me. My Grandma lived close to the land. Even through enslaved lineage and being a sharecropper, she still loved the land. She grew flowers and vegetables up until she was 95 years old. She was born in 1901 and died when she was 109 years old. With a third-grade education, she was the wisest woman that I ever knew. I loved her, and I knew she loved me. I respected her, and she respected me. I carry her wisdom with me to this day. My grandchildren, Julian, Paisley and Quinn belong to this lineage. I want to hand to them what my grandma handed me. I have more privilege, agency and means than my grandma had, so I must give. This is my way of paying it forward. These excursions are about love, memory, healing and the strength to keep going.

These state park adventures have not been easy though. Even after going into standard remission from Multiple Myeloma, I faced relentless challenges. Over the last two years, I endured bouts of pneumonia, bronchitis and sinusitis. I was bedridden often, on monthly rounds of antibiotics and steroids throughout 2023 and 2024. I suffer from spinal degeneration, which makes walking difficult. Fortunately, with the help of an incredible nurse practitioner and pulmonologist, Amy Wilson, we discovered I had eosinophilic asthma. Once treatment began, I could finally breathe again. I also receive regular epidural shots in my neck and back—not to erase the pain, but to make movement possible. And still, through all this, I persevered. We went out yonder.

Julian, at ten, is a little more reluctant to go on our trips than when he was five. But once we're out there, in the woods, by the lakes, away from screens and distractions, he opens up. He skips rocks. He scouts for mushrooms. We do not pick them. We just identify them. Julian hunts for rare insects. He becomes a seeker of wonder.

Then came Hurricane Helene. While we were safe, my mother and my brother Willie (visiting from New Zealand) lost power, surrounded by storm damage. We became mission-driven of a different sort. We drove to a café downtown. Dressed in dinosaur pajamas, he helped me gather hot food, coffee and soup. then navigated backroads filled with downed trees and live wires to deliver comfort. We called it "the assignment." He was brave in his dinosaur pajamas. I was proud.

In the wake of the storm, I had a reading scheduled at Conestee Nature Preserve. I expected it to be canceled, given the devastation, but Erin Knight insisted that I come. "People need the uplift," she said. So I went—and I brought my mother. As the sun set, I read poems into the dusk. That evening held a kind of quiet magic. Though Conestee is not a state park, I include the Kwansabas. I wrote "Deeply Rooted" for the nature preserve. Like every other place Julian and I visited, the Conestee speaks of nature's resilience—and ours.

Ultimately, this book is not only about South Carolina's state parks. It is about a relationship between a Gaga and her grandson. It is about memories made, and love lived in trying times. It is about hope showing up in unexpected places. There were moments I doubted we'd finish. Moments when Julian seemed to lose interest.

But then, out of the blue, he would walk into my room and ask, "What park are we going to today?" I'd try to hide my surprise, pack up the car, and then off we went to King's Mountain State Park. From the mountains to the coast, we found something special at every state park. We finished the mountain and coastal parks first. I expected less from the Midlands, but the joke was on me—they turned out to hold beauty and magical wonders, too. Each park gave us something to hold onto.

I had no idea the impact our journey would have on others. After a poetry reading of *The Song of Everything* in Pendleton at The Bookshop, a man about my age came up to me with tears in his eyes. He told me, "You taught me something." He said, "I am becoming an Ultimate Outsider, but I never thought to bring my grandsons. These books I am buying are for them. I will be taking them with me from now on." You never know who needs the message of multi-generational going together. I am happy to offer these poems, these treks of exploration and inspiration. There are deep joy, sorrow and revelations in this book. Yet, like the first one, it is weighted with themes of historical racism and present-day racism. These encounters resonate on a personal, familial and collective level. The pain is still held in the land. African Americans had to fight to be allowed to access the state parks. This fight was present at the very beginning.

When Julian and I journey to each and every park, it feels like a reconciliation of sorts. We go not just for ourselves. Again, I showcase the Kwansaba poem, an African American form, in this book to frame my gaze at the parks. In *Over Yonder*, I am pleased to offer a poem form that I created, the Afro Carolina Quilt Stitch—an eight-line poem divided into four couplets to honor my lineage, especially my foremothers.

As I write this foreword on March 23, 2025, Table Rock is on fire. These are precarious times. My answer is to keep going in the face of fires, hurricanes, hate and illness. We do not know what is around the bend—literally and metaphorically. I say, go Over Yonder! There are good people everywhere. There is a message nature has for you. Find your Pocket of Joy in the midst of the struggle. Julian and I are Ultimate Outsiders now—but really, we are just a Gaga and Grandson who dared to wonder and wander together and found healing in nature.

— *Glenis Redmond*
Poet Laureate of Greenville, SC

This Wild Verdant Now

Gaga and grandson still hand in hand
on this *Ultimate Outsider* status quest we
sought on this five-year trek. Cancer,
still a river runs through me but
doesn't staunch our flow. Julian spins out
of control every once in a while, but
we find our bearings. We press on.

Oh, how we press on. Foot after
foot on forest floors. One after the other.
We look back. We look ahead but see
the beauty in this wild verdant now.
We're shifted and shaped by twists and
turns. The trees sing to us. They're
not the only ones busy with growth.

Over Yonder, Directions

"Follow the old ways," Grandma always quipped.
"Yes ma'am," I'd reply as if I
knew what she was talking about.
Grandma had her ways, and they did
not include many words. So I'd watch
her. She kept close to the land
as if it held all the answers.

To learn how to listen takes time.
Some think it only takes the ear,
but it's the heart in sync with
earth, wind and water. I tell myself:
Lose the noise. Empty your whole self
of grief, doubt, fear, anger and hurt.
Find your well. Fill it with goodness.

Grandma pointed and said, "Over Yonder."
Like always, I didn't quite know what
she meant, but I heeded her wisdom.
Went out there. Made my way. She
knew one day I'd absorb the wisdom
of her command. Round the bend. Be
right where I was meant to be.

Rites of Passage
Lake Greenwood

They came to me through the river
in deep strong pulses. Waves.
At first, I didn't know the source.
One day I got quiet and turned
inward. Knew then that all my mothers
with their hands one after the other
washed over me. I came into myself.

Fisherwoman and Child
Lake Greenwood

Grandma could not swim a lick, but
she fished in lakes all the same.
With her cane pole in hand, she
casts for Crappie and Croker. "Best fisher
in the county," Mama boasts. She grows
mythic in my young mind, a can-do
woman down by the water reeling in.

The Story I Never Heard
Lake Greenwood

At just age ten. Mama hated fishing.
Grandma said, "Cook. Supper. When I'm done.
Skip the fishing. Deal?" Lil Nette nodded.
Her Mama would fish all day. Would
come home with a mess of fish
or none, still got a warm meal.
This is how Mama learned to cook.

First Generation College Student
For Sadlers Creek State Park

I'm 61, but my girl self weeps
at the water's edge. I knew she
would've loved to come to this park
as a student at Erskine College, but
she was busy tearing down barriers.
Would rather been here 32 miles away.
Sun soaked. Finding herself. Poetry circling around.

Wild Thing: I've Always Been Green

Note. I've always been a nature lover.
A tomboy much to my mother's chagrin,
"What to do with that girl child?"
A tree climber. Child of the woods.
What you'd expect, Mama? You got what
you named me: Glenis Gale, a valley
wind, a force that can't be tamed.

Unexpected Back Seat Counselor

In the backseat, after taekwondo,
Julian asks: "Gaga, do you still have cancer?"

"Yes, baby, I do,
and I will always have it."

"Is there treatment
that will take it away?" I tell him,

"There's a place in Mexico, that claims
they can treat my kind of cancer, but
it costs $50,000. I don't have that."

"When I grow up," he says,
"I'm gonna send you there.

Where do you hurt the most?"
"My back," I answer.

"Then that's where I am going
to have them focus on first.
I will start with regeneration
to cure you.

I love you."
"I love you," I reply.
"I know you do." I pause,
letting his words settle.

"Julian, thank you
for opening my car door,
and for holding the door
at the beginning of class.
It meant a lot. You are a gentleman.
I see you."
He smiles through the rearview mirror:
"I told you, Gaga.
I love you."

Name the Good
Hunting Island State Park

Julian and I escape
our 2,200-square-foot living
in the Upstate for a beach trip every year.
This summer almost passes us by,
so we go on a Labor Day weekend trip.
We pack the car, head south
to the Lowcountry, reach Lady's Island
just when the orange and pink
take over the sky.
We say our revelatory *oohs* and *ahhs*.
Julian says something like,
"God's busy painting."
I stare at him and think,
he is my grandson.
With his way with words.

We breathe the salted air deep,
shed four hours of Upstate travel.
We take our shoes off, walk on the beach,
let the waves speak to us.
We note the seabirds.
We are so glad we've made it,
but really, we are the mile markers.
He's nine-years-old, about to turn 10 in a week.
I just turned over the page from 60.

The next day, I expect more magical moments,
but the bright light of day is startling.

Before we hit the sand,
we need breakfast.

I brought some of Julian's favorites,
but he needs protein.
I fry up the bacon,
but it is not the right brand.

He only eats specific brands.
It's the smell and the taste—
not picky, but food aversive.
Julian only eats 15 foods. Sum total.

I am reduced to tears.
I have failed.
I just want him to be nourished.

While trying to make him eat,
I flash back to when
I toured the country doing poetry,
stayed at a bed and breakfast in Jackson,
Mississippi.
I refused to eat breakfast,
but I learned from the owner:
you don't skip breakfast at a B&B.
It is in the name: Bed and Breakfast.
It's what they do—
it's in the title.

The owner told me,
"Sit down and eat."
I obeyed. She continued,
"I want you to go out into the world fortified."
Her words felt like a huge warm embrace.
Isn't that what we all want for our loved ones?
To feel safe and held.

I want Julian fortified.

We had snacks galore for the car trip,
Baked Lays potato chips (only in the small bag),
Veggie Straws (only in the party-size bag),
Boar's Head Deli meat (Genoa Hard Salami),
a plain bagel with butter (from Starbucks).

In my haste, I should have packed more food.
Should've. Could've. Would've.
But we are in this moment now.
We are both hangry.

I look at Julian and myself.
Feel I have fallen short as a Gaga.
He looks at me and says,
"It is not your fault.
It is not your fault, Gaga."

He is trying to tell me
of the mechanism
that ticks within him.

This makes me cry even more.
He looks at me and says,
"Gaga, you see only the bad."
I wipe my eyes. Take a deep breath,
"You're right, Julian.
Let's name the good. You start."
Julian says, "We are here."
This beautiful big-eyed boy
becomes my teacher.
We sit side by side on the couch.
I say, "Shells and orange Lantana."
He says, "Frogs and stars."
I say, "Seagulls and terns."
He says sandcastles
and the whole ocean
We go on and on.
Our trip turns with our
name-the-good gaze: "Cumulus clouds."
Or, "Look how the lake reflects the clouds."
Or, "There's an ice cream stand
on the side of the road. Let's go."
He gets the multicolored Superman flavor.
I get salted caramel.
The rest of the trip
is not without conflict,
but everywhere we turn—
we find our path back
to each other.
We become cartographers
naming the good.

What Julian Thinks About Parks

Gaga says, "Come on let's go. We go."
When I go out into nature,
I become more alive,
and my brain relaxes.
I swing on swings.
I go down slides.
Go across creeks. Bare feet.
Sometimes I throw rocks in the lake.
We look for birds like cardinals.
We look at plants, especially mushrooms.
Then on Gaga's app, we look to see
if they're poisonous or not.
We learn their names.
We know to not eat them.
We wouldn't anyways.
Gaga and I go to parks
because she wants
to spend time with me.
At the park we both become
more calm.

The Reluctant State Park Traveler

Where are we going? To the park,
on one of our state park adventures, Julian.

I don't want to go.
But you said you did. I do...
but can I bring my iPad? Family Time,
remember?
Can I bring Mama's spare phone? No devices.
Oh, okay...
Let's go. Just a minute.

Thirty minutes later.

Julian, glad you're in the car.
Are we there yet? Not yet.
Are we there yet? Not yet.
Can we stop and get snacks?
Sure, we can get whatever we want.

We grab chips, candy and water. We're back
on the road.

Julian shouts, Gaga, look at the mountains!
Look at the clouds!
I'm driving, but yes—wonderful.

Gaga, we're finally here! This is so cool.
Shoes off, splashing,

Julian turns to me with a smile
as wide as the ridge of the mountains.

Says, "Best day ever, Gaga!"
I take in the expanse
of the moment.
Exhale.

Inland
  For Sadlers Creek State Park

I thought I knew creeks, small streams
running over a bed of rocks making
a trickle, tinkle that plays like music
to the ear. A song that calls.
Sadlers Creek. Stood me still with awe.
I tried to take it in. Seemed
more like an ocean with endless waves.

We Were Not Ready for the Beauty
Kings Mountain State Park

My I-85 drive-by
does not do the park justice.
Anytime, I could have turned right;
anytime it was waiting for me.
I cannot tell you how many decades
I missed pulling into the welcome arms
of the oak, the sweet gum and the red maple,
the calling of the lake
and beckoning rolling hills.
The quaint old farmhouse,
the creek and the autumn
golden and rust leaves
falling into the water.
Julian and I walking the wooded trails—
transported to our quieter selves,
walking on boulders
across the creek.
Become some version
of our younger selves.
We zoom in on—
insects, flora and fauna.
Our conversation falls
to hushed tones,
hand gestures. Points
Come here,
Look at this...
Look at that...
And this.

The Quiet, That's Not So
After Joy Harjo

The country is so quiet—
except for the lyric in the bush.
The chorus of birds. The chime of the Wrens.
The picture that the museum of Starlings
paint.
The magic the Marlins cast.
The charm of Hummingbirds.
The gulp of Swallows.
The serenading rain.
The sharp clicks of crickets and cicadas.
The wind-woosh.
The gale shudder.
The thunder.
The leaf rifle and dance.
Wave slap.
The honking horns of the geese.
The high-pitch annoyance of mosquito.
The funeral call of the Mourning Dove.
Their haunting coo.
The astute owl's questions: Who? Who? Who?
The frog bleep.
The Crow caw—
or the yip of their ancestral call.
The cheep and chirp.
The skitter and scamper of paws and claws.
The growls.
The bizz and beep.

The fish-plop. Flip. Flap and flop.
The gnat's zizz. Zazz.
The woodtapper.
The buzzy bee zapper.
The tree crack and creak.
The peep and peep.
The zip and zap of dragonfly.
The pitter patter on the pond.
The lake.
The stream.
The gurgle and glug.
The constant thrum of a drum.
The here and there.
The everywhere.
All at once and then
sometimes not at all.
Silence. Silence. Silence.
Then, the music begins again.
Then, the symphony.
The groove.
The funk in this song.
Then the lull.
To just sit in it.
To dance to it—
in splash of creeks and waterfalls.
The washing over us all.
It washes over us all.
And that is all
and that is everything.

C is for Cumulus Clouds
For Lake Warren State Park

We, Capricious Cartographers,
find Comfort in these Cushions of Calm—
Chalk Chambers. Congregations of Cotton
Characters.
Compelling Clutter. Cusps of Cake.
Coveted Charisma.

We say, Cumulus. Cumulus. Cumulus.
They obey the Command and Come.
We climb into the clouds.
Take delight in their Cyclical Conversations
as we find Community in their Countenance
and Copious Consolations.

We coo as we spy Celestial Cliffs,
Creamy Canopies, Colossal Castles,
Cherub Choirs and Cargo of Cloud-born
Calamity.
Choruses of Cathartic Civilizations.

There's a Crow. There's a Carolina Wren,
a Cow with what else? A Cowbell.
There's South Carolina. Our whole Country
and there's my Cool Cousin Christine.

In Consensus, we take note
of Concurrent Cantatas
with our Cultivated Canons.
We peer through the Cryptic Curtains.
We name every Colloquial Curly Cue.

Then, from our mouths and minds,
let them Cascade away
like dreams. Like Chariots.

I'm With the Black Lady, a Found Poem
Pleasant Ridge Negro State Park

"The Forestry Commission considered
numerous sites
before the land for Pleasant Ridge was found.
The most promising location for a colored park
was the Blythe Property, a 200-acre tract
twenty miles south
of Greenville on Highway 25."

Joseph R. Bryson, a U.S. Congressman
from the Fourth District of South Carolina,
received a protest letter from several residents
of Pelzer:
"It will be the most demoralizing thing
that can happen to our community,"
wrote a woman who owned a farm near
the property.

A woman from Newberry whose old home
adjoined the Blythe Property insisted that this is
"one of the finest white communities in the state
This is something we cannot accept.
We will fight like the opponents of Camp
Buckhorn."

"A Black lady from Greenville appealed,
Sometimes it is necessary
to overrule local requests
for the public good and
do what is right."

"Pleasant Ridge State Park became
the only entirely separate black state park
in the South Carolina park system.

The Greenville County Legislative Delegation
requested that there be no publicity
about the Highway 11 purchase
until the land was acquired."

What to Do in Water
Pleasant Ridge State Negro Park, 1954

"Don't get in that water,"
the adults sing,
but the July heat bears down,
so boys do what boys do,
be how boys be—
hardheaded, bent on fun.

The park,
not quite a full park yet,
not up to code,
not up to standards,
but it's 1954 we take what we get,
and it was all we had.
Separate but hardly equal—
not so great again,
but better than before.
A place for us to gather,
to relax.
Church outing.
Cookout—
a long way to travel—
a youth group from
New Pleasant Grove Baptist Church
in southern Greenville County.

I'm sure of the splash. Splash and romp.
The dare.

The sinkhole and whirlpool.
The mad dash.
Safety had come and gone.
One foot too far.
Cries for help.
If they could swim.
If Ed Grant, 16.
If Curtis Arnold, 14.
If Roosevelt Johnson, 14.
If there was a lifeguard on duty.
If they had swim classes.

If they could have arced
their lithe bodies
and poised their arms
into a purposeful stroke,
or kicked their feet
into the less graceful dog paddle.

If they knew how—
to just let go—
not struggle,
not fight the ripples
of their own making.
If they could raise their heads
not sucking down brackish water,
pulling their bodies to be sinking stones.

If they could just trust
the water would hold them
like God's clear palm—
relinquish their
beautiful Black backs
to the creek.
Floated. Eyes to the sky—
they'd rise
to the surface,
drift to the shore,
breathing
thankful air,
grateful,
weary, wore out,
but alive.

Somewhere to Lay My Head
Poinsett State Park

Goes one of my favorite Gospel songs.
Words wrung out of need. Black park
workers worked. Worked until weary
but could not sleep on a park
bed, only a stiff cot rented for fifty
cents in the colored quarters. Lay down.
Fold arms. Legs. Rest wouldn't be easy.

Touchstones
for Julian

I want to remember—
every beautiful moment,
every intense one too.
I want to go back and see them,
each etched in Love.
Every time,
I pocketed a stone.
When my fingers slide
over a sleek round rock
or jagged edge,
something lands within me.
I see you out the corner of my eye—
doing the same,
a collector too.
You too know the secret powers
stones hold.
I was once a quiet girl,
and I gathered stones,
and they told me stories
no one else could tell.
They spoke with the mouths
of the ancestors.
I'd take some home
to line the windowsills of my bedroom,
let them continue their telling—
they would whisper,
wail and sing.

They have been here
long before us,
speaking of what came before,
of the people
who walked this way
before we did.
Julian, there are times
my mind slips in and out.
I cannot discern
if it's old age
or what the chemotherapy
has left of my mind,
but I want to keep walking this way
with you
as long as I can—
and when my body folds,
and my spirit flies away,
I want you to keep walking.
Find stones to hold.
Let them talk to you.
Remember what they say
of our times and times before us.
Remember for us both, grandson.
Remember for me:
We. Were. Here.

Deeply Rooted
for Conestee Nature Preserve

You'll never know how much you need
to be here until you are. Walk.
Round the bend, where the yellow Parsnips
and pink flowers bloom. The meadow opens.
Glows at dusk. In this rare light
the Oaks stretch wide. Take you in.
Stand still. Behold. Be held. Exhale. Be.

We come to this land to behold,
to be held by Conestee's green palm.
The giant Red and Water Oaks bid
us to circle 'round and listen to
stories on top of stories that nature
tells. We become deeply rooted to the
past and to the beauty here now.

The first stewards still walk the land—
you can almost hear the Hendersons busy
with their doings. Put hand to ground
and feel the drum and thrum—music
of the grist mill, but nature is louder:
The Running Water chants its holy hum.
Here we come to be filled. Healed.

There's so many animals to spy, yet
the winged ones I favor the most:
the gaggle of geese with their horns,

and the bright red suited cardinals, dotting
the trees. Too many birds to count.
Each day a new cast of colors.
And a host of others join in.

Helene blew through, but we're still here.
As in our lives, we take stock.
Tote heavy loads. Elders say, "Many hands
make light work." Or, lighter. Not just
the light from the sun and moon
but from each other's strength. We link
to these deep roots, and we climb.

One to another is always the answer.
Nature, forever the teacher, tells us to
take heed. Knows all in due season.
Green or gold. Mist. Fog, shine
or rain. When the field is fallow,
do not let the eye mislead you.
Beneath us, life dances in the dark.

We rarely think of them. Roots. But
they're there. Silent in their deep mission.
Anchors. Doing the work: pushing up what
needs to be held down: Trees. Plants.
Us. Some people root us too—
May we do the same for others.
Spur growth. Inspire each other to rise.

Sometimes You Just Gotta Go
Hickory Knob State Park

Even though you need to purge the clothes closet.
Even though you need to do three loads of laundry.
Even though you need to do taxes.
Even though you need to make doctor
appointments—for yourself and others.
Instead, you unhinge yourself from the endless
to-do list.
Get a pen. Circle a pine tree on the state park map.
Jump in the car. Throw worries out the window.
Ride the road, where the rubber makes music with
the road
where the waves carry you up and over to a place—
you standing on firmer
richer ground.

On Finding Oconee Bells
Devils Fork State Park

Down the trail and around the curve
by the water's edge. Kneel. Put eye
and heart to ground. Find that girl
donned in a white ruffled dress. She
rings and sings out to all who
sit still long enough to listen
to the secret stories that she holds.

There's Always Sky
for Paisley and Quinn

Daughters of my daughter,
Paisley and Quinn.
Your Gaga writes to you.

This is my wish:
Let the light be light
as long as you can keep it.
By light, I mean joy—
Yellow and sunshine-bright,
like your giggles.

May you find it daily,
the way you teach me
not to dwell in shadows,
unless it's in play.

Dear Quinn, stay curious.
Spy ladybugs—
as you say, *madybugs*—
on ground level with ants and beetles,
animals and caterpillars.
Butterfly.

Dear Paisley, stay enchanted,
with your eyes trained
on the power and beauty of flowers—
dandelions and roses.

Paisley and Quinn,
what I am saying to you:
May you always stay lit
by the wonders nature holds for you.

May you keep that part
of you alive and safe.

May you always hold
on to nature.
It can be one of your
greatest friends.

May you always go into the forest.
See the trees and know them by name:
Willow, Oak, Redwood, Loblolly Pine.
May you love them as I love them—
as much as I love you.

May you not only be a tree hugger,
but remember you come
from a long line of tree climbers:
your Mama and Auntie Amber—

unafraid of the ascent.

I would look out the kitchen window
and see those little ones
high in the branches,
chattering like birds for hours.

I would not scold them
like my mama did me—
Girl, get down from that tree!
I was queen of tomboys,
wild hair and dirty knees.
I was free.

I was a little girl too—
climbing trees,
sitting among the leaves,
feeling at peace.
Feeling at home
when the world got too much.

And to the two of you,
I hope you will always be free.
Free enough to go out into the forest
to find yourself—
or to just have fun.

Climb trees, chatter with the birds
like your Mommy & Aunt Amber
your loving Poet Gaga
out on limbs.
May you seek our counsel
and the counsel of trees.
May you Climb.

Remember who you are.
Remember where you come from—

a long line of women
who defy.
Dare to dream, climb.

Paisley and Quinn,
May you too remember:
whatever or whomever
tries to hold you down—
always look up.
Continue to climb.
Remember
there's always sky.

Keynotes

You shut the door, but the wide
world waits. It's not what are you
hiding from, but who. Go. Face
who you are afraid to face. You.
Give your grief to the ground. Know
it can hold the weight. Release your
woes. Between you, the river and sky.

Mayfly Lesson

A death sentence comes for us all.
Some lives stretch out—lyrically long.
Others a dash—poignant, but short.
The point is—we don't know,
the cadence or our death date—
whether we live 1 day
or 21,915 days or more.
Let's not count, but make
each moment add up—
feathers to our precious lifespan.
While we can, let's flit.
Be. Free. The best we can.
In this meantime.
Let us fly as we may.

Sew and Sow
Afro-Carolinian Quilt Stitch #1

Give Mama her flowers while she's living, even
though she sings: *Every duck*

praises its own pond. I believe you praise your pond
only if it raises you

to higher more tender heights. Mama sewed and
sowed into me, so this too is how I tend to

my flock: a knowing look, inspiration, a jewel of
affirmation. Sometimes I wanted to get there fast,

so I went alone, but really, I was always carried by
the many who made me into this body of water.

There's a tributary flowing from my pen: *This little
light of mine, I'm gonna let it shine.*

May you praise your own pond if love be there and
may you be praised in return. May you gather this

beauty. May you in turn touch backs and bid those
backs to sprout wings.

TIMELINE FOR SEGREGATION AND ACCESS IN SOUTH CAROLINA STATE PARKS

1930s–1940s: The CCC and the Creation of State Parks

· South Carolina's state parks were largely developed during the New Deal era through the Civilian Conservation Corps (CCC).

· These parks were created for white visitors. Black people were allowed in only as laborers— not as equal citizens seeking recreation.

1942: Opening of Myrtle Beach State Park

· One of the earliest state parks, it—like all others—was whites-only in policy and practice.

1950s: "Separate but Unequal" Parks for Black Citizens

· In response to civil rights lawsuits, South Carolina created three segregated "Negro parks":

  - Pleasant Ridge State Park (Greenville County)

  - Mill Creek State Park (Sumter County)

  - Hickory Knob State Park (temporary designation)

· These parks were poorly funded, lacked adequate facilities and operated only seasonally or briefly.

1960: The Penn Center was one of the only sites in the South to accommodate biracial groups.

By the early 1960s, The Center hosted such notable civil rights leaders as Dr. Martin Luther King Jr. and Andrew Young. In the early 1960s, South Carolina native and civil rights activist, Septima Clark, conducted several citizenship workshops at the Penn Center for the Southern Christian Leadership Conference (SCLC)." The Penn Center's staff often involved itself in civil rights controversies. In 1963, The Penn Center published a pamphlet, titled the "Public Parks and Recreational."

1963: Court Rulings Pressure Integration

Federal courts began ordering desegregation of public recreational facilities across the South. Rather than integrate, South Carolina closed many of its parks entirely, citing "maintenance."

1963–1973: Palmetto State Park Closed for 10 Years

Rather than comply with integration, the state shut down Palmetto Park for a full decade. This act reflects the extreme lengths to which the state went to preserve white-only spaces.

1970s: Gradual Integration

Parks slowly began reopening and accepting Black patrons, though often without formal acknowledgment or apology. Many Black families still did not feel welcome or safe returning to these spaces. More initiatives and programs have to be instituted to make Black families feel that the South Carolina State Parks belong to them too.

1980s–Present: Reclamation and Representation

Though no formal reparative actions have taken place, Black families, artists, and historians have begun reclaiming their place in South Carolina's outdoor narrative. *Over Yonder* is part of this reclamation—offering visibility, honoring legacy, and amplifying the stories of African Americans. There is more storytelling to do. Tell the stories and tell them whole.

ACKNOWLEDGMENTS

I want to thank the indomitable and ever-creative Lib Ramos of Good Printed Things for her thoughtful and intentional collaboration on the South Carolina State Park Books both I & II. Her vision to make them a box set—complete with a journal for park-goers to use to write their own inspired thoughts, prose, poetry or doodle was lovely. This work would not be in the world without her guidance and attention to detail. Bravo again to Alexander Rouse for the cover illustration. I simply adore his work and can think of no better match for *The Song of Everything* and *Over Yonder*. His renderings capture the soul of both books.

Thank you to Camille Dungy for her leadership and for her groundbreaking book *Black Nature: Four Centuries of African American Nature Poetry*—the first anthology to bring African American environmental poetry to national attention. That collection shaped me. Her words of direction, and her lovely foreword to *Over Yonder*, are deeply meaningful to me.

Thank you to Ashley Crout for her editorial skill—her immense joy for grammar, poetics and lyricism. I am in awe at both her wit and thoughtful eye to detail. She knows when a poem is not finished and is not afraid to tell me so. She helped to corral these books into shape.

To my mother, Jeanette Redmond, who continues to inspire me with her stories—she mentions one thing about the past, and I'm off, digging deeper into history. With her words washing over me, I wade into the water. I cherish and honor my grandmother, Katie Latimore, in these pages. She kept showing up again and again. Though she never visited a state park, she was an outdoors woman who loved to fish at Lake Greenwood, tend her garden and live by "the old ways"—by hand and close to the land. I think of her often on my park adventures, especially when I'm on a dock in the Lowcountry and see Black folks fishing. In their posture and presence, I see her. She had only a cane pole, a cigarette often hanging from her lips, but she would've been right there—fishing for solace, for quiet, for connection. I believe my outdoor ways come from her. I know my grandmother loved and respected me, and I her. I would drive past cotton fields from Erskine College to get to where she lived in Laurens just to sit with her a spell. With only a third-grade education, my grandmother was a master class in living. I have known none wiser, except a close second—her daughter, my beloved Mother.

Thank you to my grandson, Julian "Seidon" Priester—my first grand—for riding along with me on these escapades. He doesn't know how much I needed his ride-along. He was my lifeline after my cancer diagnosis. We took to the road. Even while facing his own struggles, I have watched him rise again and again. He is a brilliant, bright human with a mind like a finely-tuned machine and the heart of a poet.

Thank you to my daughter, Amber Sherer, for allowing us these treasured times together. I thank my granddaughters, Paisley and Quinn Farmand, for being bright nature beings who inspire me on our walks and play. I hope to do a North Carolina State Park adventure with them next. Thank you to both their Mother and Father and Celeste and Christopher for giving me Gaga time with them both.

To the Baldwin for the Arts Residency—thank you for the time and space to write. Some of these poems were born there. To the City of Greenville for embracing me as its inaugural Poet Laureate—my programming with you has shaped my thinking about green spaces in powerful ways.

Additional thanks to my daughter, Celeste Sherer—thank you for your thoughts about state parks. Your first job as an interpretive guide at the Carl Sandburg Home showed me your gift as a storyteller. You even took me behind the scenes to the slave cabins not included in the tour, knowing your Mama loves the "story under the story," as Lucille Clifton writes.

Thank you to Stephen Lewis Cox and his dissertation on Negro State Parks in South Carolina. It provided facts and many uncomfortable truths that help set the context for the state park books.

I extend gratitude to the South Carolina State Parks for making space for these books on their gift shop shelves. Thank you to the Greenville Public Library for carrying the books, and to M. Judson Booksellers for hosting a reading and showcasing the series. To Paris Mountain State Park—thank you for holding your first-ever poetry reading with *The Song of Everything*. It was deeply meaningful, especially with Amber and Julian there, as well as my nephew Brock Redmond, his wife Aryele Carter Redmond and their baby son, Carter, who cooed and babbled as I read—a poet in the making.

Thank you to Erin Knight, Director at Conestee Nature Preserve—thank you for inviting me to read, even after storm Helene. That small gathering reminded me once again that poetry is essential, soul-buffering in times of upheaval. I later wrote "Deeply Rooted", a suite of seven linked Kwansabas, and read them at the Big Blue Gathering fundraiser.

Thank you to Aldon Knight, Executive Director of Upstate Forever and fellow Erskine alumni, for inviting me to share my poetry at Upstate Forever's Green Awards.

A sincere thanks to both Black and White social justice warriors of South Carolina Park's history who battled for us all. Your work and passion made it possible for not only Julian, Paisley and Quinn to enjoy these parks but for all people to come and enjoy our beautiful parks. Your work was not in vain.

Finally, I thank the Divine—the mighty Force that I call Mother and Father God—for leading me into stillness, into pastures of peace. I thank my ancestors who walk with me daily and keep me grounded.

Though my gaze often lingers on what is unsettling, I know it also turns toward joy—for this is how I rise daily. I am grateful to live this poet's life—for its inspiration.

ABOUT THE AUTHOR

Glenis Redmond is Greenville, South Carolina's Inaugural Poet Laureate and a 2025 recipient of the Order of the Palmetto, the state's highest civilian honor, awarded by the Governor and approved by a bipartisan committee in recognition of a lifetime of extraordinary achievement, service and contributions on a national or statewide scale. She has dedicated over 30 years to a career as a poet, teaching artist and literary citizen.

Most recently, Glenis received the Highlights Foundation Inspire Scholarship in 2025 and is serving as a Baldwin Fellow (2024–2025). In 2023, she was selected as a Poet Laureate Fellow by the Academy of American Poets. She was also named a Citizen Diplomat by the Jonathan Green Maritime Cultural Center.

In 2022, Glenis received the Governor's Award for the Arts and was inducted into the South Carolina Academy of Authors, the state's literary hall of fame. She is a Cave Canem alumna and a veteran of the U.S. Army

Reserves. Glenis earned her B.A. from Erskine College and her M.F.A. in poetry from Warren Wilson College.

Her poetry has appeared in *Orion Magazine*, *Callaloo*, *American Poets*, *The New York Times* and the *North Carolina Literary Review*. *The Listening Skin* was shortlisted for both the PEN Open Book Award and the Julie Suk Award.

Glenis is the proud mother of twin daughters, Amber and Celeste, and a devoted grandmother ("Gaga") to Julian, Paisley and Quinn.

She believes that poetry is the mouth that speaks when all other mouths are silent.

glenisredmond.com

Good Printed Things is a small press based in Greenville, South Carolina.

Since 2018, we have published works focused on connection — with ourselves, others, and the surrounding world. Specializing in small print runs, Good Printed Things works with both emergent and established writers and artists to seek out, explore and celebrate the good.

goodprintedthings.com

www.ingramcontent.com/pod-product-compliance
Lightning Source LLC
Chambersburg PA
CBHW051300020426
42333CB00026B/3289